BLOOD PRESSURE

QUESTIONS YOU HAVE...ANSWERS YOU NEED

People's Medical Society Books
Currently Available from Wings Books

Getting The Most For Your Medical Dollar

150 Ways To Be A Savvy Medical Consumer

Take This Book To The Hospital With You

Your Heart
Questions You Have...Answers You Need

A PEOPLE'S MEDICAL SOCIETY BOOK

BLOOD PRESSURE

QUESTIONS YOU HAVE...ANSWERS YOU NEED

by ED WEINER
and the Staff of the
People's Medical Society

WINGS BOOKS
New York • Avenel, New Jersey

The People's Medical Society is a nonprofit consumer health organization dedicated to the principles of better, more responsive, and less expensive medical care. Organized in 1983, the People's Medical Society puts previously unavailable medical information into the hands of consumers, so that they can make informed decisions about their own health care. Knowing that consumers, as individuals or in groups, can make a difference, the society is involved in the debate over the future of the medical care system.

Membership in the People's Medical Society is $20 a year and includes a subscription to the *People's Medical Society Newsletter*. For information, write to the People's Medical Society, 462 Walnut Street, Allentown, PA 18102, or call (215) 770-1670.

This 1993 edition is published by Wings Books, distributed by Random House Value Publishing, Inc.,
40 Engelhard Avenue, Avenel, New Jersey 07001,
by arrangement wiht the People's Medical Society, Inc.

Random House
New York • Toronto • London • Sydney • Auckland

Printed and bound in the United States of America

Library of Congress Cataloging-in-Publication Data

Weiner, Ed.
    Blood pressure: questions you have—answers you need / by Ed Weiner and the staff of the People's Medical Society.
        p.   cm.
    Originally published: Allentown, PA : People's Medical Society, c1984.
    Includes bibliographical references.
    ISBN 0-517-08902-5
    1. Hypertension—Popular works. 2. Hypertension—Miscellanea.
I. People's Medical Society (U.S.) II. Title.
RC685.H8W43   1993
616.1'32—dc20   93-2000
                                          CIP

10 9 8 7 6 5 4 3 2

INTRODUCTION

Since early 1983, when the People's Medical Society was founded, the volume of requests for information has been staggering. Clearly, consumers have an unquenchable thirst for knowledge about specific medical conditions or ways to safely and successfully negotiate their way through the medical world.

One of the conditions about which we have been asked the most questions is blood pressure. Why are people writing to us seeking information about high and low blood pressure when there is already so much written about them? It's because much of the blood pressure literature available for public consumption is written from a limited and often self-serving perspective. For example, if the information is produced by a pharmaceutical company, blood pressure-controlling medications have a tendency to take center stage. Or if the information is written by a medical doctor, modes of treatment by nonphysician practitioners may be overlooked or ignored.

Our goal, then, was to create a document that would make no prejudgment as to whether one form of treatment was better than another. Instead, our approach is to give you all we can gather, the good news and the bad. We point out serious problems with very routine and common forms of treatment. We suggest ways you can act to help control the problems associated with high and low blood pressure.

We chose to present the information in a question-and-answer format. The questions are those we are most often asked. The answers are based on recent research available from all sources. We tried to order the questions in as logical a way as possible, but to make it easy for you to find a specific answer to a specific question there is an index at the back of the book.

Throughout the text you will find certain words in bold type. Those words appear in the glossary at the end of the text. This is to help you cut through the technical jargon and better understand the condition and its treatments.

Finally, a bibliography gives you good leads if you want to get into more depth on specific aspects of the condition.

Every People's Medical Society publication is designed to give medical and health care consumers the information they need to choose their own course of treatment or care. I believe *BLOOD PRESSURE: Questions You Have . . . Answers You Need* fulfills that intent.

Charles B. Inlander
President
People's Medical Society

BLOOD PRESSURE

QUESTIONS YOU HAVE...ANSWERS YOU NEED

*Terms printed in boldface in the text can be found in the glossary, beginning on page 62.

Q: What exactly *is* blood pressure?

A: It's the force of your blood's trip from your heart to and through the rest of your arterial and vascular system. When your heart beats—when that portion of your heart called the **left ventricle*** contracts—oxygenated blood is literally shot into your arteries.

In its travels through your body, your blood presses against the walls of the blood vessels it's passing through. The vessels stretch and contract to maintain blood flow. If the vessels are narrowed, increasing the resistance to blood flow, blood pressure rises.

When it comes to measuring blood pressure and expressing it in numbers everybody can understand, there are two sets of readings.

When the left ventricle contracts, and the blood's force against the vessel walls is at its greatest strength, you have what is called **systolic** pressure. After that contraction, when the heart is more or less in its resting phase, the blood pressure is lower. This resting or relaxation pressure—the pressure in the arteries just before the next heartbeat—is known as the **diastolic** pressure.

Blood pressure readings, then, come in two numbers. For example, 120/80 (expressed as "120 over 80") or 150/95, and so on. The first number is the systolic, while the second number is the diastolic. The difference between the two readings is known as the **pulse pressure**.

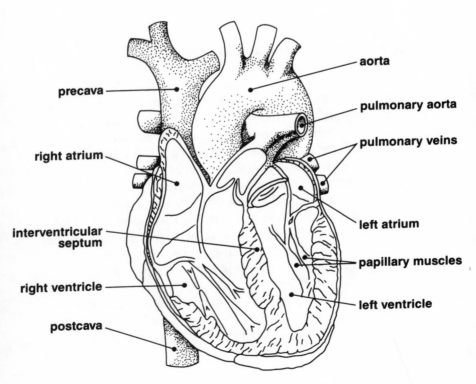

Q: Which of the blood pressure numbers is more important—the systolic or the diastolic?

A: Both are of interest and concern to doctors, but the one they seem most interested and concerned about—the one that starts the bells ringing and the lights flashing—is the diastolic.

Q: What is normal blood pressure?

A: "Normal" is always a relative term when it comes to the way human beings function. Taking body function measurements isn't like taking a history exam: There aren't any "correct" answers and no "perfect" scores. A lot depends on a whole host of conditions.

According to prevailing wisdom, a reading of about 120 systolic over 60-90 diastolic is "normal." But you'd be hard pressed to find anybody with exactly 120/80 pressure, or with exactly 120/80 all the time. The 120/80 measurement is an average of a pretty wide range of readings. Various times of the day, activities, or emotional states can raise or lower the reading without being a sign of anything wrong.

Q: How do you get those numbers—120 over 80, and such—anyway? And what's "mm" and "Hg"?

A: Those numbers are derived from readings taken with the standard blood pressure measuring device, called a **sphygmomanometer** (pronounced *sfig-mo-muh-nom-i-tur*—it's a toughie, all right). If you've ever had a physical examination, you've met up with a sphygmomanometer. Most people refer to it simply as a **blood pressure cuff**.

The way it works is this: A wide band, or cuff, is wrapped around your upper arm. The cuff is then inflated by air pressure. At the same time, the air pressure pushes a column of liquid mercury (Hg is the scientist's abbreviation for mercury) up along a numbered scale that is measured in millimeters (usually abbreviated as mm).

A stethoscope is placed against your arm's artery, known as the brachial artery. When the cuff has been inflated enough to cut off circulation to the lower part of the **brachial artery**, the person listening through the stethoscope (which is placed against the artery at the crook of the arm) will hear no sound. As the pressure is slowly released, the cuff loosens, the blood begins to flow again into the lower artery, and the column of mercury falls. At the point when the stethoscope can pick up the tapping of the heartbeat in the artery, the millimeter level of mercury indicates a figure approximately equal to the systolic pressure. Soon, as the pressure in the cuff is further released, the beating sound disappears. The number on the millimeter scale at that point is approximately that of the diastolic pressure.

So if your blood pressure is 120/80, or 120 mm Hg/80 mm Hg, what that means is that your systolic pressure was detected, pinpointed, and measured when the column of mercury was at a height of 120 millimeters, and your diastolic pressure was detected, pinpointed, and measured when the column of mercury was at a height of 80 millimeters. The numbers merely represent a convenient method of noting and comparing blood pressures.

Q: Are blood pressure readings with a sphygmomanometer accurate?

A: They're close but not perfect. While other, more accurate measurement methods exist, they are far too complicated and invasive for general office or home use. For the most part, a sphygmomanometer reading is actually somewhat lower than the true arterial pressure.

Another problem with this indirect method of determining blood pressure is that you can get incorrect readings if you don't do the procedure just right. For example, if you don't pump the cuff tight enough—and, thus, don't entirely collapse the brachial artery—you'll get a reading that's too low. The same goes if you let the air out too quickly, or if you use an adult-size cuff on children or grownups with very thin arms. You might get a false high reading if a person's arm is too thick for the standard cuff. That's why some obese people who don't have high blood pressure seem to—it's not their blood pressure, it's the inadequate size of the cuff that's providing the false reading. And your home reading could be way off if you take your pressure with your arm resting on a table or in some other such elevated position—the cuff ought to be at heart level, and the best way to do that is if the arm is kept down at your side.

In today's booming self-care market, most new, low-cost blood pressure measuring devices are not the mercury column type of sphyg-momanometer. Instead they have gauges or digital readouts. While the mercury column types are still considered the best, most accurate, and most durable, they are a bit more complicated to use without help and they are more expensive. The new kids on the blood pressure block can do well enough if they are, first, well-made and, second, taken care of. And, perhaps, occasionally serviced, if possible.

And don't forget to ask your health practitioner if his or her sphygmomanometer has been checked for accuracy and serviced lately. Incidents of office sphygmomanometers being way off—and thus affecting treatment options—is more common than you might think.

Q: When is a blood pressure reading considered high blood pressure?

A: Again, it's a fuzzy area. According to the medical experts, when blood pressure remains at 140/90 over a period of time (usually at least two readings over three days, or after several hours' rest) in people under 40 years of age, that's **high blood pressure**, or **hypertension**. In people over 40, 160/95 puts you into the danger zone. The reason you need to have your blood pressure measured several times over a few days —or even a couple of times in one visit—is that nervousness, real or imagined intimidation by doctor or staff, stress, or any number of things can raise your blood pressure momentarily. To go with a single reading would not take into account blood pressure's normal, everyday ups and downs.

Labile hypertension is the name given to this fluctuating kind of high blood pressure. **Sustained hypertension** means you have it all the time. Labile can become sustained if not taken care of.

Q: Is high blood pressure a disease?

A: Definitely.

Q: What causes it?

A: Here's an answer you're going to hear a lot during the course of this book: Nobody knows for sure. It may be due to one thing, or it may have "multifactorial etiology"—scientists' lingo for lots of different causes and reasons. Heredity is one factor, although that only explains transmission, not cause. Diseases of the kidney are prime culprits. The brain chemical acetylcholine has been linked to hypertension, as has something called the natriuretic hormone. **Sleep apnea**—a sudden stoppage of breathing during the night—may cause high blood pressure in older men (although it might be the other way around; nobody knows for sure). Environmental conditions have also been implicated. It could be all or one or none—always, sometimes, or never. That's what makes high blood pressure so tough to fight and to make generalities about— and to write inflexible prescriptions for.

Q: Is high blood pressure a common disease?

A: It sure is. Somewhere around 61 million people, give or take. But only about half of those who have it know they have it.

Q: How can people not know they have high blood pressure? What are the symptoms?

A: That's the point—there are hardly any symptoms at all. And when those few that do exist turn up, it's usually only after the blood pressure is very high already. That's why they call it the silent killer. It's one of nature's little jokes on humans, but about the only way to know if you have high blood pressure is to find it out when you have your pressure checked. Or when you keel over from a stroke. That's the drastic way of finding out—it won't help you very much, but it'll answer your next of kin's questions.

For the record, the American Heart Association provides these heart-stopping statistics:

High blood pressure is implicated in many of the deaths and disabilities resulting from strokes. Strokes killed 150,300 people in the U.S. in 1988. Nearly 31,000 more lives were lost because of high blood pressure or hypertensive disease.

Sixty-eight million Americans have one or more forms of heart or blood vessel disease.

In 1988, the latest year for which complete statistics are available, an estimated 982,574 deaths were caused by heart attack, stroke, and related diseases. That's more than double the number of deaths due to cancer.

Q: You mean, there are absolutely no symptoms?

A: Well . . . there are very few absolutes these days. What might be possible symptoms of high blood pressure vary from person to person, and they could be symptoms of other health problems as well. But . . . most doctors say that if you're having headaches, heart palpitations, a flushed face, blurry vision, nose bleeds, a tough time catching your breath after exertion, fatigue, a strong need to urinate often (especially during the night), **tinnitus** (a ringing or buzzing in the ears), **vertigo** (feelings that you or the world is spinning dizzily), or any combination of these— well, then check your blood pressure to see if that's the problem.

Q: Can high blood pressure be cured?

A: Well, yes and no. **Primary** or **essential hypertension** (85 to 95 percent of all cases) is the kind of high blood pressure that seems to happen, either because of heredity or other unknown or hard-to-find factors. This kind of hypertension doesn't have a cure, but it is controllable through various means and procedures that we'll talk about soon. Essential hypertension is a by-product of one or several glitches in the body's system of checks and balances that regulates pressure in the arteries.

Secondary hypertension occurs as an offshoot of some other condition, very often kidney disease. (The kidney, in terms of high blood pressure, can be either culprit or victim; that is, it can either be kidney problems that cause the high blood pressure or high blood pressure that causes kidney problems. Either way, the renal [kidney] system is among the first to be considered when hypertension is present.) By controlling or curing the basic problem, secondary hypertension may just disappear.

Q: What can happen to me if I leave my high blood pressure undetected and untreated?

A: You could find yourself being referred to in the past tense. Besides the aforementioned stroke, high blood pressure is a nicely paved highway leading to heart attack, congestive heart failure, or coronary artery disease, and other high speed exit ramps from this life. By making the heart work harder to push blood through the vascular system, high blood pressure—in the form of **hypertensive heart disease**—can make the heart grow in size and at the same time tire it out, with unhappy consequences. Further, it's believed that the increase in blood pressure eases the way for fatty deposits to build up on the artery walls and eventually clog them.

Reducing hypertension pays off in big ways. A recent study of 37,000 people, reported in the British medical journal *Lancet*, found that for every five to six points that a person's blood pressure is reduced, the risk of heart disease declines by 20 to 25 percent and the risk of stroke by 30 to 40 percent.

Q: **When the doctor tells me my high blood pressure is "benign" or "mild," does that mean I don't have anything to worry about?**

A: What it means is that your hypertension isn't **accelerated** or **malignant**, two extremely serious stages of the disease. However, as pointed out in the textbook *Principles of Internal Medicine*, "Hypertension is never truly benign, since even mild elevations of diastolic pressure are associated with increased risks of premature death and of vascular complications involving eyes, brain, heart, and kidneys."

Q: **Are men more likely than women to have high blood pressure? Blacks more than whites?**

A: According to most research, hypertension occurs almost twice as frequently in blacks as in whites, and blacks suffer more illness and death from their elevated blood pressure. High blood pressure can be found more often in white men under 50 than white women of the same age, but after 50 it's just the reverse; among blacks, there is no difference in occurrence between men and women. About a quarter of all whites over 65 have high blood pressure; the percentage is 50 percent for blacks.

Q: Is blood pressure affected by the weather? By the changing seasons?

A: As a matter of fact, it is, for certain people. If you have normal blood pressure, there's no seasonal variation. However, according to researchers at the department of medicine and geriatrics of Osaka University Medical School in Japan, people with essential hypertension can expect slightly higher blood pressure in winter than in summer. The reason given for why this happens is complicated and mere educated guessing.

Q: During a physical examination, my doctor looked in my eyes to see if I had high blood pressure. How come? What could he see?

A: It's because high blood pressure causes changes in the **retina**—from constriction of the **arterioles** to more serious bleeding and optic damage. The retina is the only place in the human body where the arteries and arterioles can be looked at directly. And as a result of a retinal examination a medical practitioner can gain a lot of information about which stage of hypertension a person is in and what needs to be done. The worse the changes in the retina, the worse the prognosis.

Q: Does blood pressure go up when you get older?

A: It doesn't have to, but it often does. And when it does, it's frequently related to **arteriosclerosis** —"hardening of the arteries"—which affects the elasticity of the arteries, the flow of blood through them, and the increased pressure on the more rigid vessel walls. Arteriosclerosis and **atherosclerosis**—the most prevalent form of arteriosclerosis and the major cause of stroke and heart attack in the United States—are trademarks of high blood pressure and a dizzying spiral to ill health, because not only does high blood pressure lead to the development and worsening of arteriosclerosis and atherosclerosis, but the worsening of these diseases then can lead to higher blood pressure readings. Blood pressure going up with age might also be related to the weight we put on as we get older.

While a certain changeability in systolic pressure is to be expected—in extreme cases, systolic pressure balloons up past 200 mm Hg in about 1/10th of all older folks—diastolic pressure should not change with age.

Q: Can nervousness raise my blood pressure?

A: It can, especially if it's a long-term nervousness, or what is normally called psychological stress.

What happens, it seems, is that life's pressures cause the kidneys to retain sodium—but only if you're at high risk of developing high blood pressure in the first place (because of family history or a current high-normal blood pressure). Combine this with a person's sympathetic nervous system tending to react in an exaggerated way to stress, and you've got a clear path ahead to blood pressure troubles.

Q: Isn't stress primarily a problem of the workplace?

A: Not at all. Home pressures, family problems, money problems, even excessive noise are all stressful situations that can lead to high blood pressure and cardiovascular disease. And even game-playing stresses can do it—blood pressure can rise like a guided missile while a person is playing a video game. At least one video game-related high blood pressure death is on record.

Q: If stress is my high blood pressure problem, what can I do to unstress myself?

A: Your doctor might put you on antihypertensive medication and let it go at that, or perhaps urge you to exercise to work off your nervous energy.

On the other hand, certain kinds of behavioral therapies have been shown to work. Deep-breathing relaxation training, in combination with diet and sodium reduction, has allowed many people to go off their medication completely with no risk. Biofeedback is another technique of tuning in to the body's own calming rhythms that's met with success, as has progressive muscular relaxation.

Meditation is a well-known relaxer, and studies performed and reported by researchers employed by Maharishi International University—the think-tank arm of the Maharishi Maheshi Yogi's transcendental meditation movement—claim that the meditators' systolic blood pressures are significantly lower than the blood pressures of same-age nonmeditators.

And studies show conclusively that owning a pet, or merely watching fish swim in a tank, can do wonders for your blood pressure health.

Behavioral therapists certainly can be recommended by your physician. The other forms of relaxation may not exactly be your doc's cup of tea. You can probably get a lead on these other techniques, and others, by asking at your neighborhood Y, or checking out the Yellow Pages.

The Chinese knew about behavioral therapy for high blood pressure long before it had a fancy medical name like hypertension. Ancient Chinese doctors recommended "placidity under

all circumstances." It's a theory that works as
well today as it did back then.

Q: Can people with high blood pressure exercise safely?

A: Not only can most high blood pressure sufferers
exercise safely, but the exercise can bring their
blood pressure down. You just shouldn't overdo,
although a physical education instructor at the
Pennsylvania State University has shown that
hypertensives not on medication can exercise
moderately—walking, jogging, or swimming—
even in temperatures up to 100 degrees
Fahrenheit. The exercise ought to have weight
loss as its goal.

It's tough to say for sure if exercise alone
lowers blood pressure. The drop could be the
result of exercise-induced weight loss or a change
in body sodium levels. But that's for scientists
to argue over. Just so long as it does something
good, it's worth the doing, even without
knowing all the whys and wherefores.

Aerobic exercise benefits cases of mild and
moderate high blood pressure, but it's been kind
of a no-no to do **isometric exercise**. The
pushing, grunting, and straining of the isometric
resistance routines have been viewed traditionally
as blood pressure elevators. However, newer
studies are indicating that, yes, blood pressure
might go up at the beginning, but the long-term
effects are those of blood pressure reduction.
Have a long talk about an exercise regimen with
somebody who knows—a qualified fitness
instructor, for example.

Q: Are there any exercises to absolutely avoid?

A: We wouldn't recommend the marathon, at least not right off the bat. And the blood pressure-raising strain associated with weight training is pretty much a no-no. Remember, moderation is the key.

One piece of equipment to avoid if you have moderate to high blood pressure is the inversion bar and shoes, or antigravity boots, as they are sometimes called. What you do with this gear is simply hang upside-down. It's supposed to be good for the spine and the body's musculature, and some aficionados love doing gut-ripping situps and other calisthenics while dangling from the bar like a bat. Inversion therapy's bad news, however, even for healthy, nonhypertensive types. After only three minutes of this suspended inanimation, people with normal blood pressure have readings of 150/100.

Q: If I have high blood pressure, do I have to give up driving?

A: Probably not. The research into this area hasn't been able to pick up any real long- or short-term health hazards for the hypertensive. So, rev 'er up . . . but be sure to buckle up first.

Q: And how about sex?

A: Yeah, how about it! Sexual intercourse has a great elevating effect, not the least of which has to do with blood pressure. Systolic blood pressure levels can shoot up a whopping 107 percent, diastolic up as much as 60 percent, and heartbeat a'pounding up to 120 percent faster than usual. Some people have had coital blood pressure coming in at 300/175 mm Hg, or 237/138 on the mean for men and 216/127 for women. The peak is reached at orgasm; less than two minutes later, blood pressure has receded to levels lower than those before sex. Higher levels are hit when sex is had with a new or unfamiliar partner—opening night jitters, apparently.

Look, we can't tell you what to do—every case is different, and people have different needs and priorities. Some people can handle it, others are in real danger of going out in a blaze of glory. Your health care professional can best answer your questions about how safe having sex is for you. Good luck.

Q: I'm a smoker. Should I stop if I have high blood pressure?

A: You should stop even if you don't have high blood pressure, but especially if you do. There's enough evidence to point an accusing finger at smoking as one of the major risk factors in the development of high blood pressure, and as a bad guy in accelerated cardiovascular disease.

Studies have shown that while no one knows for sure exactly how tobacco smoke causes vascular disease, it's pretty clear that smoking causes the body to release more **catecholamines** into the system. Catecholamines are chemicals the body produces in response to stress. They make the heart beat faster and with greater force, and cause blood vessels to constrict, among other things. This increase in cardiac output raises the blood pressure. Smoking speeds up release of the hormone **vasopressin**, and this too elevates blood pressure.

Researchers at the University of Southern California School of Medicine showed that if a person inhales nicotine-containing smoke, the production of **prostacyclin**—a chemical that dilates, or expands, the openings of blood vessels —is reduced. By doing so, nicotine smoke is directly involved in higher blood pressure and, perhaps, more extensive coronary heart damage.

And if that isn't enough to get you off your butt, yet another study, this from the cardio-vascular center of New York Hospital-Cornell Medical Center, outlined a connection between smoking and blockage of the kidney's artery (**renal artery stenosis**, to use the technical terminology). What the scientists found was that of those who were suffering from renal artery stenosis, all had significantly higher systolic and diastolic blood pressures, and 94 percent of the men and 74 percent of the women were smokers.

Finally, yet another recent study showed that nearly three-fourths of women who had been hospitalized for malignant hypertension were smokers and/or oral contraceptive users.

What this says, clearly, is that if you discover you have high blood pressure, giving up smoking

has got to be one of the first steps you take.
Giving it up before developing the condition is
better yet. Best of all is never smoking to begin
with. An ounce of prevention is worth a pound
of hypertension.

Q: Wait a second—you mean oral
contraceptives cause high blood pressure?

A: You bet. Progestogen, an estrogen in "the pill,"
causes the body to produce more of a substance
called angiotensin, which in turn elevates the
blood pressure. Oral contraceptives raise blood
pressure in almost all women who take them,
but more so in women with a family history of
high blood pressure or those with a history of
hypertension during pregnancy.

If there's any good to be said about all this,
it's that "pill"-produced high blood pressure is
usually reversible—all you have to do is stop
taking the oral contraceptive. A study in England
found that women who had stopped using the
pill for at least a month had blood pressures
similar to those women who had never used
the pill.

If you plan to take the pill, it's a good idea to
have your blood pressure measured ahead of
time. If it's already high, it may be wise to
explore alternate methods of contraception. If
your blood pressure is normal before using the
pill, doctors suggest checking your pressure
regularly at home or at least every three to four
months at the doctor's office for the first year

of use. If everything's okay at that time, a semiannual checkup ought to do the trick. If everything's not okay, you probably ought to stop using the pill.

Q: Well, now that I know that smoking and the pill are probably bad for my blood pressure, what else do I have to look out for?

A: If you drink alcoholic beverages, you might want to reconsider the ways you wet your whistle.

Q: You mean you're going to take booze away from me, too?

A: No. You have to take it away from yourself. The evidence is fairly strong that those who tipple may topple.

When 4,783 men and women 20 years of age and older were studied by a team of scientists at the University of California at San Diego to see how drinking affected their blood pressure, the results (published in the journal *Hypertension*) indicated that as little as the equivalent of two stiff belts a day (30 milliliters of alcohol, or slightly less than an ounce) was all it took to produce a "modest but consistent" increase in both systolic and diastolic pressure readings. The researchers noted that men 35 years of age or older downing that amount of booze were nearly twice as likely to have high blood pressure as nondrinkers. And the direct correlation is clear: Blood pressure was especially high if those examined had had alcohol during the previous 24 hours.

According to a doctor working with the Stanford Heart Disease Prevention Program, by increasing alcohol consumption from one to three drinks per day in men 50 to 74 years old, systolic pressure would rise just as much as if the body weight of those men had increased from 165 to 195 pounds. He also offered the theory that if you have at least one or two drinks a day, and if you also have high blood pressure, and if you're over 50, you should try abstaining for a while—your blood pressure could go down, thus saving you all kinds of doctors' bills and unnecessary medication costs and side effects.

Exactly how and why alcohol affects blood pressure isn't known—it just does. And that's important to know.

Q: How do my eating habits affect my blood pressure?

A: What you eat—and how much—has a lot to do with where your blood pressure level resides.

As a general rule, obesity and high blood pressure go hand-in-pudgy-hand. Obesity may cause high blood pressure which in turn may cause cardiovascular disease, but—as with nearly everything in the study of blood pressure—the mechanism is not clear. In fact, it may not be there at all. Obesity and high blood pressure could be totally independent problems, merely existing side-by-side in the body of a person with heart disease. While many scientific studies show that the blood pressure of certain over-weight people drops when those people drop some poundage, other studies have indicated that the hypertensive obese person may not be in any greater danger of heart attack and heart-related deaths than a nonobese hypertensive—and, in fact, the obese person may be in less danger. Others say that weight loss without antihypertensive drug therapy at the same time may have no real and lasting effect on individuals with mild hypertension.

Still and all, it probably pays to lose weight, whether or not it shows up immediately on your blood pressure scorecard. Besides looking and feeling better, you probably will live longer too. According to the Society of Actuaries, if you are 30 percent above average weight, your risk of dying from coronary disease, compared with people of average weight, is 44 percent higher for men and 34 percent higher for women. Whether that has to do with blood pressure is moot—and irrelevant, really. It has to do with living, and that should be sufficient motivation.

Q: Are there any specific foods to stay away from?

A: Well, you might want to at least cut down on coffee and meat, if not cut them out entirely.

For years debate has ensued on whether coffee, or caffeine intake, has an elevating effect on blood pressure. Early studies from Duke University and Harvard Medical School said it was a sure thing. The Duke study, especially, drew a clear connection between caffeine, high blood pressure, and stress; it showed that a few cups of coffee can raise blood pressure, and when work-related stress or everyday pressures were factored in, the mixture wasn't good, especially for java-gulping, tense office workers. Wrote the Duke researcher in an issue of *Psychosomatic Medicine:* "Blood pressure increases of the magnitude seen in the present study could potentially eliminate or reverse the therapeutic effects of a number of the anti-hypertensive medications currently in use." A more recent study—this one of more than 45,000 men by researchers at Harvard University School of Public Health—exonerated coffee as a heart risk factor. The researchers reported in the *New England Journal of Medicine* that men who drank even as much as four cups of coffee a day had no higher risk of developing heart disease than those men who drank no coffee at all. For some folks, then, a moderate amount of coffee, but not an excess, might be okay. For you? You might want to try it both ways—with coffee and without—and see how your blood pressure reacts.

As for meat eating, it too has been linked to increased blood pressure. A few studies demonstrating that connection may have been tainted because they looked at how vegetarians (who often have better blood pressure readings than omnivores) reacted to meat—never thinking that part of the observed blood pressure rise was the result of anxiety of non-meat-eaters eating the stuff. However, at least one newer study took "regular" eaters, put them on a veggie diet, watched as blood pressures dropped, put them back on their usual meals, and saw their blood pressures go back up again.

You needn't feel obliged to become a total vegetarian, but cutting down on meat is probably a good idea.

Q: Anything else?

A: Uh-huh. Cut down on fats. When you need to use them, use the polyunsaturated kind, like safflower, sunflower, corn, olive, and canola oils (they may have a diuretic effect). Eat mackerel, rainbow trout, haddock, and Atlantic salmon occasionally (they contain large amounts of eicosapentanoic acid—EPA—which is postulated to have a beneficial effect on blood pressure and cardiac health in general). Increase your intake of dietary fiber.

Q: Which foods are high in dietary fiber?

A: So glad you asked:

Foods High in Dietary Fiber

Food	Portion Size	Grams of Fiber
100% bran cereal	1 cup	19.9
Baked beans	½ cup	8.3
Apple	1 medium	7.9
Broccoli, cooked stalk	1 medium	7.4
Spinach, cooked	½ cup	5.7
Almonds	¼ cup	5.1
Kidney beans	½ cup	4.5
Cabbage, shredded, boiled	½ cup	4.3
Shredded Wheat	1 cup	4.3
Peas, cooked	½ cup	4.2
White beans	½ cup	4.2
Banana	1 medium	4.0
Corn	½ cup	3.9
Potato	1 medium	3.9
Pear	1 medium	3.8
Lentils	½ cup	3.7
Lima beans, cooked	½ cup	3.5
Sweet potato	1 medium	3.5
Pinto beans	½ cup	3.1
Peanuts, chopped	¼ cup	2.9
Brown rice, raw	¼ cup	2.8
Cornflakes	1 cup	2.8
Oats, rolled	½ cup	2.8
Orange	1 medium	2.6
Raisins	¼ cup	2.5
Brussels sprouts	4	2.4
Peanut butter	2 tablespoons	2.4
Whole wheat bread	1 slice	2.4
Apricots	3 medium	2.3
Carrots, raw	1 medium	2.3
Beets	½ cup	2.1
Peaches	1 medium	2.1
Kale, cooked	½ cup	2.0
Zucchini, raw	½ cup	2.0

Sources: Adapted from

McCance and Widdowson's *The Composition of Foods,* by A. A. Paul and
   D. A. T. Southgate (Elsevier/North-Holland Biomedical, 1978).
Nutritive Value of American Foods in Common Units, Agriculture
   Handbook 456 (U.S. Department of Agriculture, 1975).
"Composition of Foods Commonly Used in Diets for Persons With
   Diabetes," by James W. Anderson, Wen-Ju Lin, and Kyleen Ward,
   Diabetes Care, September/October 1978.
Composition of Foods: Soups, Sauces and Gravies, Agriculture Handbook
   8-6 (U.S. Department of Agriculture, 1980).
Composition of Foods: Spices and Herbs, Agriculture Handbook 8-6 (U.S.
   Department of Agriculture, 1980).
"Topics in Dietary Fiber" and "Fiber Analysis Tables," Reports of Research
   of the Cornell University Agricultural Experiment Station, 1978.
Information supplied by cereal companies.

Q: And what about salt? That's supposed to be bad for me, isn't it?

A: Well, as we've been seeing, nothing's easy to say for sure when it comes to blood pressure. And the subject of salt in the diet is another uncertainty that's grown into a full-blown controversy—one that's been brewing for nearly 80 years of blood pressure research.

To start off with, the mineral sodium is necessary for human well-being. Sodium is a part of many foods and food additives. Salt is 40 percent sodium, and salt is the vehicle by which most of us get our daily portion of sodium. The problem is this: Our daily portion is just too high. We only need 200 milligrams a day, but most of us are sopping up as much as 30 times that amount.

Most of us don't have any adverse reaction to sodium. However, it's likely that there is a large minority percentage of people who are genetically programmed to react to sodium by having their blood pressure rise.

If we have learned anything in this book, it is that nobody knows for sure the mechanism for anything that has to do with blood pressure— and the sodium-high blood pressure connection is no exception. Some scientists believe that blood pressure goes up in the people in which it does go up because sodium increases water retention, and the result is greater arterial pressure. But that's just conjecture at the moment.

There's no real controversy about salt/sodium in some way causing high blood pressure in people genetically susceptible to sodium's effects. The brouhaha has to do with the idea that by cutting back on sodium via low-salt diets, all Americans can avoid getting high blood pressure. There is no clear evidence that that is actually the case.

In other words, salt will more than likely raise your blood pressure if you already have high blood pressure (although this won't happen in all hypertensives), but it won't necessarily raise your blood pressure if you're normotensive (have blood pressure in the normal range).

Q: So that settles it, huh? Salt's not so bad after all?

A: Remember, in Bloodpressureland, nothing is ever settled . . . except, perhaps, estates. Everybody's got a theory, and the guns on one side are as big and respectable as those on the other. Take, for example, this quote from the chancellor of the University of Tennessee Center for Health Sciences: "In the absence of proved need or benefit and because of the potential harm, excessive sodium consumption by the American public is a justified cause for concern." Or here's one from the chairman of the department of physiology at the University of Maryland School of Medicine, who calls the sodium-high blood pressure link "dangerously minimized."

Or look at the research from a study conducted in the Netherlands that involved newborn babies. Half of the group of infants was put on a normal-sodium diet for the first six months of their lives, while the rest of the kids ate a low-sodium menu. Results: The normal-sodium babies developed higher blood pressure than the lower-sodium group, leading the doctors conducting the study to conclude that blood pressure is related to sodium intake, and that "moderation of sodium intake, starting very early in life, might perhaps contribute to prevention of high blood pressure and of rise of blood pressure with age."

And other studies come to the same conclusion.

Q: So who's right and who's wrong?

A: Possibly everybody's a little right and perhaps everybody's a little wrong . . . maybe.

Q: It's all so confusing! What's a person to do?

A: A concerned person will be careful, not overdo, and eat smartly. The person with high blood pressure will go on a low-salt diet and see if that helps. It could help so much that further therapies, including antihypertensive drugs, will not be necessary, especially if yours is a mild hypertension, and you couple salt/sodium reduction with weight loss.

The person with normal blood pressure will control the urge to salt everything—just in case. Besides, food tastes better without the salt. It tastes like itself. That's not to say you should abstain, or put yourself through the hell of a bland diet. A low-low-salt diet is not only frustrating—eating tasty food is one of life's great pleasures—but it also ensures the urge to cheat, indulge, binge and, perhaps, pay the consequences . . . whatever they may be. Listen to your body; heed what it says to you; act—and eat—accordingly.

Q: Besides keeping the salt shaker off my table, what else can I do to restrict the sodium in my diet?

A: Here's what:
- Watch for the "hidden" sodium in canned, frozen, or otherwise processed foods. Canned vegetables often have salt added to them. Even canned fruits may have salt in them.
- Don't go to all the trouble of keeping the shaker invisible while dining—then go and add salt to soups, stews, etc., while cooking. It does the same damage (that is, if it does damage). And make sure the same goes for when you eat out. All your willpower at the table can be for naught if the chef is going hog-wild with the salt in the kitchen, or is using flour with high sodium content, along with sodium-laden baking powder and baking soda. And if you're in a Chinese restaurant, be aware that the food is often liberally spiced with monosodium glutamate (MSG), and this popular flavor enhancer has a high sodium content. Furthermore, don't add soy sauce or tamari to the food—both have lots of sodium and "hidden" MSG in them.
- Certain antacids are high in sodium, although in recent years new lines of antacids have been developed that are lower in sodium than their older cousins. Always check the label.
- Naturally occurring sodium can slip into your tum unbeknownst to even the most scrupulous dietitians. One of the sneakiest is milk (120 milligrams per cup). Celery, artichokes, and spinach have moderate amounts of sodium, too.
- Some drinking water may have a lot of natural sodium in it, but studies are inconclusive

when it comes to whether it raises your blood pressure significantly.

- Be sure you understand the language of low-salt. In Food and Drug Administration-specified terms, "sodium-free" means less than 5 milligrams of sodium per serving; "very low sodium" means 35 milligrams or less per serving; "moderately low sodium" means 140 milligrams or less per serving; "reduced sodium" means the usual level of sodium has been cut by at least 75 percent; and "unsalted," "no salt added," or some equivalent phrase refers to food once processed with salt but now produced without it—although the food may contain other forms of sodium.

- Become expert at fixing your meals with spices that will make you forget that there is even anything called sodium. For example:
  —On eggs, try dill, oregano, or chopped chives, individually or mixed together.
  —For mashed potatoes, boil the potatoes with a clove of garlic, mash the potatoes, add chopped parsley, cayenne pepper, paprika, dill, or curry powder.
  —Season vegetables with nutmeg.
  —Rub chicken with garlic, sprinkle with lemon juice, and dust with paprika, sage, and thyme.
  —Rub red meats with fresh ginger and add rosemary or crushed black pepper.
  —Dump out the salt and fill the shakers with oregano, basil, thyme, caraway seeds, sesame seeds, or poppy seeds.
  —Other spices to experiment with are allspice, chili powder, curry, ground mustard, peppermint, tarragon, coriander, cardamom, cumin, cloves, and celery seeds.

Q: Any other things good for me to eat for my high blood pressure?

A: Besides what's been discussed already, there are three major pieces of dietary advice: calcium, magnesium, and potassium. Foods rich in these three minerals—and high in their ratio to sodium—are generally conceded to be blood pressure lowerers and heart protectors.

Let's take calcium first. Results of a Cornell University Medical College study point to the importance of calcium in the workings and the therapy of hypertension. Other research—and there is a good deal of it—has shown that hypertensives eat less calcium than normotensives; that when as many as 17 different nutrients were examined, it was only the calcium level that separated the high blood pressure sufferers from those with normal blood pressure; that a group of people without high blood pressure who added one gram (1,000 milligrams) of calcium to their daily diets had drops in their diastolic blood pressures; and that some scientists think that the way doctor-prescribed diuretics lower blood pressure is by increasing serum calcium levels. The evidence that calcium is an antihypertensive, when taken at daily levels of about 1,000 to 1,500 milligrams, is pretty convincing.

Foods High in Calcium
(And Low in Sodium)

Food	Portion Size	Calcium (mg)	Sodium (mg)
Swiss cheese	2 ounces	544	148
Yogurt (skim milk)	1 cup	452	174
Yogurt (low-fat)	1 cup	415	159
Milk, skim	1 cup	302	126
Milk, low-fat	1 cup	297	122
Tofu	4 ounces	145	8
Blackstrap molasses	1 tablespoon	137	19
Collards, cooked	½ cup	110	18
Kale, cooked	½ cup	103	24
Mustard greens	½ cup	97	13
Watercress (chopped)	½ cup	95	33
Almonds	¼ cup	83	1.5
Salmon, fresh	4 ounces	79	60
Chick-peas, dried	¼ cup	75	13
Broccoli	½ cup	68	8

Sources: USDA Handbooks 8, 8-1 and 456; U.S. Department of Agriculture Nutrient Data Research Group, 1983.

Q: And magnesium? Is that as effective as calcium?

A: Yes. Study after study from all over the world shows that daily doses of magnesium, either through supplementation or in the diet, can keep blood pressure in its place.

The accompanying list offers most good food sources of magnesium. But, depending on your diet, you might feel that you need a supplement to be certain of getting at least the recommended daily allowance of 350 milligrams a day for men, 300 milligrams for women. And, if so, keep in mind that magnesium works best when accompanied by about two times as much calcium. Also be alerted to the fact that so-called soft water has fewer minerals in it than the "hard" kind—and magnesium is among the missing. If your drinking water supply is "soft" or softened, you might want supplementation all the more—because of the process involved, sodium levels are elevated in softened water, and studies show greater amount of heart disease among soft water-imbibing communities.

Foods High in Magnesium

Food	Portion Size	Magnesium (mg)
Soy flour, full fat	½ cup	180
Tofu (soybean curd), raw	½ cup	127
Almonds, unblanched	¼ cup	105
Black-eyed peas, dried	¼ cup	98
Soybeans, dry	¼ cup	98
Wheat germ, toasted	¼ cup	91
Cashews	¼ cup	89
Brazil nuts, unblanched	¼ cup	79
Swiss chard, cooked	½ cup	75
Rye flour	½ cup	74
Whole wheat flour	½ cup	68
Peanuts, dry-roasted	¼ cup	64
Walnuts, black	¼ cup	63
Peanut flour, defatted	¼ cup	56
Oatmeal	1 cup	56
Shredded Wheat	1 cup	55
Potato, baked	1 medium	55
Blackstrap molasses	1 tablespoon	52
Beet greens, cooked	½ cup	49
Lima beans, baby, boiled	¼ cup	49
Spinach, raw, chopped	1 cup	44
Salmon, sockeye, canned	4 ounces	44
Kidney beans, boiled	½ cup	40
Avocado	½	40
Banana	1 medium	35
Pecans, halved	¼ cup	35
Milk, skim	1 cup	28
Brown rice	½ cup	28
Peanut butter	1 tablespoon	25
Beef, round, lean	3 ounces	24
Buckwheat flour, light	½ cup	24
Chestnuts, roasted	½ cup	24
Collards, cooked	1 cup	22

Source: *The Complete Book of Vitamins and Minerals for Health* (Rodale Press, 1988).

Q: And potassium?

A: Same story. Diets high in potassium seem to aid in the reduction of high blood pressure, particularly hypertension that's also connected with sodium intake. Israeli scientists announced, after a goodly amount of research, that they felt that it was potassium that was the key antihypertensive agent in the vegetarian diet.

There are various theories as to how potassium works in keeping blood pressure down; nobody knows for sure, but it's felt that it acts as a diuretic, moving excess water from the blood vessel cell walls. In this way, it's an antagonist of sodium, which works hard as a water retainer. So lots of food scientists believe that foods high in potassium and low in sodium are crucial for blood pressure control.

Here's a list of foods with a high potassium-to-sodium ratio, along with one that's vice versa. Note that canned and frozen foods aren't on the first list; that's because the canning and freezing processes change the potassium-sodium ratio in a negative way. For some eye-opening examples, see the list of processed foods.

Foods High in Potassium
(And Low in Sodium)

Food	Portion Size	Potassium (mg)	Sodium (mg)
Fresh vegetables			
Asparagus	½ cup	165	1
Avocado	½	680	5
Carrot, raw	1	225	38
Corn	½ cup	136	trace
Lima beans, cooked	½ cup	581	1
Potato	1 medium	782	6
Spinach, cooked	½ cup	292	45
Squash, winter	½ cup	473	1
Tomato, raw	1 medium	444	5
Fresh fruits			
Apple	1 medium	182	2
Apricots, dried	¼ cup	318	9
Banana	1 medium	440	1
Cantaloupe	¼ melon	341	17
Orange	1 medium	263	1
Peach	1 medium	308	2
Plums	5	150	1
Strawberries	½ cup	122	trace
Unprocessed meats			
Chicken, light meat	3 ounces	350	54
Lamb, leg	3 ounces	241	53
Roast beef	3 ounces	224	49
Pork	3 ounces	219	48
Fish			
Cod	3 ounces	345	93
Flounder	3 ounces	498	201
Haddock	3 ounces	297	150
Salmon	3 ounces	378	99
Tuna, drained solids	3 ounces	225	38

Sources: USDA Handbooks 456 and 8-1.

Foods High in Sodium
(And Low in Potassium)

Food	Portion Size	Potassium (mg)	Sodium (mg)
Salt	1 teaspoon	trace	2,132
Soy sauce	1 teaspoon	22	1,123
Bouillon cube	1	4	960
Hard cheeses			
Parmesan	2 ounces	53	1,056
American	2 ounces	93	812
Brie	2 ounces	87	356
Muenster	2 ounces	77	356
Cheddar	2 ounces	56	352
Colby	2 ounces	72	342
Swiss	2 ounces	64	148
Cottage cheese (2 percent fat)	½ cup	110	561
Snack foods			
Pretzels, thin, twisted	10	10	1,008
Saltines	10	34	312
Potato chips	10	226	200
Peanuts, roasted salted	¼ cup	243	151
Processed meats			
Salami	3 ounces	170	1,043
Bologna	3 ounces	133	981
Frankfurter	3 ounces	136	1,003
Canned soups			
Chicken noodle	1 cup	53	1,049
Cream of mushroom (prepared with water)	1 cup	94	967
Tomato	1 cup	247	816
Vegetable beef	1 cup	162	896
Canned vegetables			
Beets	½ cup	142	200
Corn	½ cup	80	195
Lima beans	½ cup	188	200
Peas	½ cup	82	200

Sources: USDA Handbooks 456 and 8-1.

The preparation of foods is crucial to the potassium-sodium ratio. For example, the potato is normally a good source of potassium—but when boiled, as much as 50 percent of it floats away . . . and when boiled in salt water, nearly half the sodium in the water seeps into the potato. Bye-bye, positive ratio.

Here's a look at various cooking preparations of a potato—and their results. As you can see, steaming is the hands-down winner.

State of potatoes	Na+ (sodium) (mmol/l)	K+ (potassium) (mmol/l)	K+/Na+ (ratio)
Raw	1	104	104
Boiled (peeled) in 1% salt	90	64	0.7
Boiled (peeled) unsalted	1	79	79
Boiled (unpeeled) in 1% salt	30	84	2.8
Boiled (unpeeled) unsalted	1	94	94
Steamed (peeled) unsalted	1	100	100

The Difference Processing Can Make

	Portion Size	Potassium (mg)	Sodium (mg)
Menu I			
Roast beef	3 ounces	224	49
Potato, baked	1 medium	782	3
String beans, fresh	½ cup	95	2.5
Whole wheat bread, firm crumb	1 slice	68	132
Unsalted butter	1 tablespoon	4	1.4
Peaches, fresh sliced	½ cup	172	1
Milk, whole	1 cup	370	122
		1,715	310.9
Menu II			
Corned beef	3 ounces	51	802
Potatoes, hash brown, frozen	1 cup	439	463
String beans, canned	½ cup	64	159.5
White bread, soft crumb	1 slice	29	142
Butter	1 tablespoon	3	140
Peach pie	⅛ pie	176	316
Milk, whole	1 cup	370	122
		1,132	2,144.5

Sources: USDA Handbooks 456 and 8-1.

Q: I have high blood pressure, and my doctor's put me on medication. My blood pressure's gone down, but I don't know how or why. What are these drugs and how do they work?

A: That's a big question and a tall order, because there are several classes of antihypertensive drugs, and each works in a different way to alter body functions in order to control blood pressure. But we'll take them one at a time and explain the basics.

Before the basics, however, there is one thing about current blood pressure drug therapy that's important to remember: Many health organizations recommend and many doctors practice a **stepped care** approach to the medication treatment of hypertension. That means that the physician who recommends drugs for the control of high blood pressure—after exploring the use of other options such as weight loss, cutting out alcohol and smoking, and the various actions we've already mentioned—will usually start off a patient with the mildest of drugs at the smallest of doses, only gradually increasing the dosage of that drug to its maximum, and then introducing if necessary another, stronger drug at its mildest dose (alone or usually in combination with the drug before it). The physician will then gradually increase this second drug to its maximum, and may move on to another type of drug and increase it until the blood pressure is at a safe level and is stabilized. It's like a series of staircases, with each flight of stairs a different drug. Once you've climbed to the top of one, you start at the bottom of the next. With any luck, and in combination with other risk-reducing activities, you might need to go only a little way up that very first flight of stairs.

And another thing to remember: Step-down is the natural goal of a step-up approach—withdrawing the stronger drugs slowly as the blood pressure level stays firm.

Q: What is the first flight? Which medication is the one to start with?

A: Ordinarily, and unless the blood pressure is dangerously high and immediate reduction is a matter of life or death, the first type of drug most often prescribed by physicians is the **diuretic**. Diuretics promote frequent urination —it's no mystery, then, why many people refer to them as water pills—which increases the elimination of water and sodium from the body, and decreases the blood volume, among other things. The diuretics most often prescribed are members of the **thiazide** family—for example, Diuril, Dyazide, and Corzide are a few of the many popular brand names—except for so-called loop diuretics, which are used for high blood pressure cases related to kidney disease.

At a minimum, 40 to 50 percent of people with high blood pressure who go on a drug regimen can control the disease with diuretics alone, and should begin to see results in six to eight weeks, or sooner.

Diuretics, *as do all other blood pressure medications*, have side effects. The most frequent unwanted results of diuretic therapy are potassium deficiency, gout, and a rise in levels of cholesterol. The potassium problem may be overcome by taking supplements in doses recommended by the physician, by reducing sodium intake, or by using potassium chloride-containing salt substitutes. Orange juice or a banana or two a day probably aren't enough to detour the deficiency, as is believed by a lot of the American public. The gout is treated with yet another drug. And the cholesterol problem is fought by keeping a low-fat diet.

Q: What's the next series of drugs?

A: In a typical stepped care step-up, if diuretics don't do the job, **adrenergic suppressants** or **inhibitors** are called into service. These include the drugs propanolol (Inderal is the popular brand name version), nadalol (or Corgard) and metroprolol (Lopressor), all three of these being in the category known as **beta blockers**; clonidine (Catapres), methyldopa (Aldomet) and prazosin (Minipress), and drugs containing **reserpine**.

Adrenergic suppressants differ from diuretics in one major regard: Whereas diuretics affect blood pressure through indirect means—by reducing sodium, water, and blood volume—adrenergic suppressants act directly on the heart, blood vessels, and sympathetic nervous system.

In general, they block the secretion of adrenal hormone epinephrine—which, when pumped into the bloodstream in times of stress, causes elevations in heartbeat, cardiac output, and blood pressure levels—and of the catecholamine norepinephrine.

There are many side effects to look for in this group of drugs. Commonly occurring are depression, fatigue, and impotence. Since there are so many side effects specific to each one of these medications, a person who is prescribed any of them ought to ask the physician or pharmacist for informational sheets on side effects, dangers, and contraindications. One should also seek out the information from the most recent *Physician's Desk Reference*, a medical manual usually referred to simply as "the PDR." It is an invaluable source of information, published annually by the Medical Economics Company, and can be found in some of the better libraries.

Q: Is there another step up?

A: Yes. The third level of drugs in a standard stepped care approach is that of the **peripheral vasodilators**, chief among them being hydralazine (popularly marketed under the brand name Apresoline). These cause the peripheral blood vessels to open for less restricted, less resistant blood flow. Again, if you find yourself being prescribed this type of medication, get a complete list of instructions, hazards, and contra-indications, and double-check with the PDR.

Q: Is that the last of the steps?

A: No. By the time you've reached this staircase, the climb has certainly brought you to the verge of breathlessness, if not weariness, and has also placed you in a group of only 5 percent of people whose blood pressures have not responded well to treatment. There are even stronger drugs, and they will surely be prescribed, alone or in concert with other types.

Q: What you seem to be saying here is that drug therapy has been the turning point in the control of high blood pressure and the saving of lives. Am I reading you right?

A: What we're saying is this: There's no question that the discovery and availability of many prescription antihypertensive medications are the reasons a lot of us are up and about today. They have played critical, life-or-death roles in the human dramas of many sick people. But they should not be placed on a pedestal or given a godlike reverence. In fact, a marked decline in high blood pressure deaths has been going on since 1940—and that's long before these drugs were even being dispensed. They are not *the* answer, just an answer, and maybe only the current answer . . . tools to be used when the machinery calls for it. And lately they're a tool a lot of doctors and scientists are thinking twice about before using.

Q: Really? Why—is there something wrong with them?

A: Well, beyond the very evident side effects involved with the taking of many of these drugs —side effects that may outweigh the benefits of the medication, or make life seem less worth the living—there is some very serious debate going on about what to take and when and for how long, and if there are long-lasting negatives associated with antihypertensive drug use.

Q: For instance . . . ?

A: For instance, the idea that's long circulated among medical practitioners that once you go on blood pressure drug therapy, you've got to keep taking those pills for the rest of your life or pay the mortal consequences.

More recently, however, some researchers have been reappraising this theory—especially in light of the financial burden placed on blood pressure sufferers by the ever-increasing cost of the drugs, and the potential toxic effects of some of these drugs as they build up in the body over the years.

And in an important study, the hypertensive-medication-for-life theory took it on the chin. The study, conducted by Northwestern University and Mt. Sinai Hospital in Minneapolis, showed that nearly two-thirds of 90 patients who were eased off their medication—at the same time that they instituted some basic life-style changes—still had normal blood pressure after a year and a half. These people had "mild" hypertension with diastolic readings of between 90 and 104. An interesting P.S. to the study is that even those whose blood pressure couldn't be held down without returning them to medication were able to maintain normal pressure with dosages lower than before the study.

A study from the Hypertension Detection and Followup Program at the University of Mississippi School of Medicine showed pretty much the same results, and concluded that mild hypertensives whose blood pressure is being controlled by one drug and who are willing to modify their diet are prime candidates for a program involving the elimination of that drug.

So, it seems, it's possible to be weaned off pressure-lowering medication with impressive results, if you're also willing to lose some weight, stop smoking, lower sodium and alcohol intake, and exercise more.

It would, needless to say, be unwise to do this on your own initiative, without first discussing the pros and cons with your health practitioner.

Q: Very interesting. What else?

A: "What else" is even more interesting—in fact, it's downright compelling.

The first "what else" is a rethinking of diuretics as the first flight in the stepped care approach. Many concerned physicians and scientists think that the diuretics are more toxic to the body's system in the long run, and create more (and, possibly, more life-threatening) adverse effects than any other antihypertensive medication; and, besides, the risk of potassium deficiency is more serious than it's often made out to be. These medical professionals are now thinking that a mild adrenergic suppressant might be better for a first, effective, and less toxic step—even though the cost to the consumer will almost certainly be greater.

But the big news is that a growing number of medical people (but still, probably and unfortunately, a minority) are joining with traditional organizations like the American Heart Association and the U.S. government's National Heart, Lung and Blood Institute in the belief that the key to therapy is not removing drugs once they've been started, but in not prescribing them in the first place—especially for people diagnosed as having mild hypertension (those with diastolic pressures between 90 and 104, a group that makes up about 75 percent of people with high blood pressure).

These doctors and researchers suggest that no studies have made strong cases for the use of drugs in what is called "uncomplicated" mild high blood pressure. What complicates matters are other cardiovascular risk factors muddying up the hypertension waters, things like smoking, diabetes, high cholesterol levels, family history, gender (males are more at risk), and race (blacks are in greater danger than whites); these factors may add up to a need for some sort of drug therapy. But for most mild high blood pressure, there's no urgency to rush into pill popping.

Your medical practitioner might not be up on his or her reading, and might not be following this latest move away from the knee-jerk prescribing. It *isn't* impolite, rude, obnoxious, or out of place to bring up these matters. After all, *you* are the one taking—or not taking—the pills.

Q: **What if your blood pressure doesn't improve after using the strongest of the drugs?**

A: Sadly, some people's blood pressure just can't be controlled, and they die from the disease. Even more sadly, a number of these deaths could be prevented because the failure is not in the drug but in the person taking it—or, rather, not taking it. In many cases, worsened conditions and fatalities are the result of people not taking their medication or not taking it in the proper manner.

If, however, a person is complying with the drug regimen and the blood pressure is still high, it is quite possibly a case of overlooked secondary hypertension, and the physician ought to redouble his or her efforts to discover the underlying physical cause of the problem.

Q: Can high blood pressure be cured surgically?

A: When kidney troubles are at the root of the problem, surgery to unblock blocked renal arteries or transplants to give the body a healthy kidney often do the job, as do other procedures.

Q: Even though a low blood pressure reading is desirable, when is blood pressure too low? And what are the dangers of low blood pressure?

A: The medical term for **low blood pressure** is **hypotension**, and according to at least one doctor, writing in the *New England Journal of Medicine*, "Hypotension is not a disease; it is an ideal blood pressure level." Furthermore, a cardiologist was quoted in the *British Medical Journal* as saying that "the distribution of blood pressure in the population is such that a small percentage of people will have blood pressures well below the mean of the general population." In fact, the Framingham study, the Cadillac of cardiovascular risk factor reports, showed that, as a general rule, the lower the blood pressure, the longer you'll live (although the risk of cardiovascular disease is, oddly enough, somewhat higher for people with diastolic pressure around 70 mm Hg than for those with diastolic pressure around 90 mm Hg).

So long as you feel well with low blood pressure, it's okay. Hypotension does, however, go hand-in-hand with various illnesses and conditions, including diabetes, **Addison's disease**, and alcoholism. You can get sudden hypotension (leading to **syncope**—fainting—or even death) after exercise—which might be an indicator of undiscovered heart problems—or after spending time in a sauna. Hypotension may accompany shock.

Orthostatic (or postural) hypotension is a condition—sometimes leading to fainting—that occurs in many people when they sit or stand up suddenly after they've been lying down or sitting for a long time, especially after a stretch in a sick bed. This type of hypotension, as well as the others, may have physical disorders as their root cause. However, they may also be **iatrogenic** in nature; that is, many people suffer hypotension because they'd had hypertension and had begun taking medication—and the medication brought their blood pressure down too low too fast . . . low enough to cause hypotensive stroke and death.

Q: When is a blood pressure reading considered low blood pressure?

A: Again, it's a smudged line, but a person with low blood pressure is probably getting persistent readings of around 100/70 or less.

Q: What can I do about my hypotension?

A: As we said, if you feel all right, you don't have to do anything. If you don't feel all right, get yourself a checkup to see if the hypotension is indicative of a hidden condition. If you're on blood pressure medication, your physician ought to look into scaling down the dosage. Ironically, you may have to do the very opposite of what people with high blood pressure do— you may be urged by your health practitioner to add more salt to your diet. If your problem is orthostatic or postural in nature, and blood doesn't reach your brain because it's pooling in your legs, you might want to start wearing tight, full-length, elastic support stockings.

Q: Are there any other, nonmedical approaches to blood pressure treatment?

A: Beyond the ones we've already talked about— diet, exercise, and behavior modification—there are a variety of methods put forth by a variety of nonphysician practitioners and alternative healers. While many of these practitioners can't produce the years of studies and double-blind experimental results that the medical professionals can, they nonetheless provide treatment —often less invasive, less costly, and with fewer side effects than traditional medicine's—that has its adherents and success stories.

It's an area of practice unfortunately loaded with charlatans and worse who are out to give unsuspecting sick and desperate people a financial soaking—but it is also an area of therapy that includes some dedicated people, some interesting ideas, and some novel approaches. But be careful: Interesting ideas and novel approaches do not necessarily make Jack a well boy. Beware of high prices, unusual and gimmicky machines allegedly designed to undo what's wrong with you, grandiose claims, and other things that smack of snake-oil salesmanship. So, caveat emptor—buyer beware—a piece of good old Latin advice, to be applied equally when dealing with medical professionals as well.

Nonphysician treatment takes in a lot of territory—from acupuncture (practiced by both M.D.'s and non-M.D.'s with some good results) to zone therapy, or reflexology, a type of treatment that uses massage of hands and feet to influence the health and function of internal organs and systems.

A number of chiropractors feel that certain blockages of nerves responsible for normal circulation can be eliminated through manipulation techniques.

Practitioners of various massage methods—acupressure and shiatsu chief among them—report that some benefit is derived from their craft, if only that of rubbing away some tension and stress.

Homeopathy, which is gaining in popularity and professional favor these days, provides reasonable, limited-invasive treatment through administration of very small doses of homeopathic drugs, salts, and elements, in the belief that a tiny amount of the "hair of the dog" that bit you will undo the damage.

Herbalists or herbologists approach the treatment of high blood pressure by prescribing doses of traditionally used flowers, leaves, and stems of a large number of plants, often prepared in the form of teas and other beverages.

Hypnotism is coming into its own as a very powerful tool. Through suggestions, much stress-related blood pressure can be eliminated. The same goes for imaging, the creation of pictures or scenarios in your mind to help you actively think the problem away via the mind-body connection. These approaches have slowly moved from the fringe to adjunct positions in the medical bag of therapies.

Doctors of so-called natural healing techniques —naturopaths—may incorporate many of the aforementioned treatments in their practices, along with megavitamin therapy and other nutritional advice. One of this discipline's long-time favorite remedies—eating lots of garlic— has been embraced (at least tentatively) by medical science as a high blood pressure curative and preventive agent.

The gentle, slightly cerebral exercise routines of yoga and tai chi help reduce blood pressure by taking the steam out of stress.

And there are many practitioners—medical and nonmedical alike—who contend that many incidents of high blood pressure are the result of food allergies, and finding and treating the allergy will end the hypertension.

It's definitely a crowded field, and a multi-faceted one. Only experience, word-of-mouth recommendations, or a good deal of background research can help you to select the method that's best for you . . . if any are. It's a field that lacks consistency—finding two practitioners in the same discipline who will prescribe the same treatment for the very same condition is difficult; they promote their own tried-and-true "sure things"—and it's a field that lacks the consistent reproducibility of results so important to making healing crafts credible. Still, people swear by them and get well by them, and that's as much or more than can be said about a lot of medical doctors.

For people unhappy with the traditional medical approach, these alternatives are available for consideration. Many of them lend themselves to continued self-care, too.

Q: So what's the bottom line on all this—by lowering my blood pressure and keeping it low, do I save money in the long run?

A: And in the short run. In addition to doctor visits, the resultant bills, lost work days, and medication costs, people with high blood pressure who don't do anything about it pay higher life and health insurance premiums. According to the publication *Medical Economics*, the premium on a five-year term life insurance policy for a 35-year-old man may be $847 a year if he's moderately hypertensive, compared with $410 if his blood pressure is normal. People with high blood pressure pay 15 to 25 percent more for health insurance. And it just doesn't make sense, since 95 percent of insurance companies say they'll lower your premium if you drop your high blood pressure to normal for up to two years.

But the real bottom line is your health—and that's something no money can buy.

INFORMATIONAL AND MUTUAL AID GROUPS

American Heart Association
7272 Greenville Avenue
Dallas, TX 75231
214-373-6300

Coronary Club, Inc.
9500 Euclid Avenue
Cleveland, OH 44195
216-444-3690

Citizens for the Treatment of High Blood Pressure
7200 Wisconsin Avenue, Suite 1002
Bethesda, MD 20814
301-907-7790

National Hypertension Association
324 East 30th Street
New York, NY 10016
212-889-3557

GLOSSARY

Accelerated hypertension: A particularly severe stage of
high blood pressure. It is considered a medical
emergency (blood pressure readings are quite high,
especially the diastolic) that is often fatal in a very
short time if left untreated. Related to kidney
disease—either as cause or result—accelerated
hypertension is a major cause of stroke.

Addison's disease: A chronic condition in which insufficient amounts of adrenocortical hormone are
produced by the adrenal cortex. Incurable but
controllable through replacement of deficient
hormones, Addison's disease symptoms include a
general feeling of weakness and fatigue, hypo-
glycemia, gastrointestinal problems, and insufficient
cardiac output. Mental and emotional problems
also result.

Adrenergic suppressant or inhibitor: A type of antihypertensive drug that acts directly on the heart,
blood vessels, and sympathetic nervous system.

Diuretic: A drug that promotes urination, thus speeding the elimination of sodium and water. This is an effective and much-prescribed method of blood pressure control.

Essential hypertension: A form of hypertension that makes up about 85 to 95 percent of all high blood pressure cases. The cause is unknown—any one of many factors, including heredity and age, may be involved together or separately in affecting the way the body regulates pressure in the arteries—and it can be controlled but not cured.

Heart attack: A popular term for a destructive, often fatal seizure involving the heart. Medical names for this "cardiac event" are *coronary thrombosis* and *myocardial infarction*. Both describe situations wherein a clot (occlusion) of some sort blocks up an artery, thus preventing blood to flow in its normal fashion. This, then, leads to the damage or death of heart muscle.

High blood pressure: See **hypertension**.

Hypertension: A disease involving persistent high readings of blood pressure measurement. In general, when readings are taken over a period of time and show blood pressure greater than 140 mm Hg systolic and/or 90 mm Hg diastolic in people under age 40, that is high blood pressure, or hypertension; in people over 40, readings of 160 mm Hg systolic and/or 95 mm Hg diastolic or higher are considered indicative of hypertension.

Hypertensive heart disease: A disorder that occurs in people with high blood pressure when the heart, forced to work harder to pump blood through narrowed blood vessels, becomes enlarged. The pumping action of the heart is affected, and circulatory failure follows.

Hyperthyroidism: A condition in which the thyroid gland functions excessively. Goiter is a common physical sign of hyperthyroidism.

Hypotension: Low blood pressure. A person is usually considered hypotensive if he or she has continual blood pressure readings in which the systolic reading is less than 100 mm Hg.

Iatrogenic: Description of diseases or conditions that occur because of the actions of a physician or another health care professional; doctor-caused illnesses are the result of iatrogenesis.

Isometric exercise: A form of physical activity and bodybuilding that involves the application of bodily force against stable resistance.

Labile hypertension: High blood pressure that fluctuates and is not persistent. If untreated, labile hypertension can become persistent and health endangering. See also **sustained hypertension**.

Left ventricle: A chamber of the heart on the lower left side. It pumps oxygenated blood into the circulatory system and body tissues.

Low blood pressure: See **hypotension**.

Malignant hypertension: See **accelerated hypertension**.

Normotensive: A term to describe a person whose blood pressure falls into normal, acceptable limits.

Peripheral vasodilators: A type of antihypertensive drug that works by opening the blood vessels to decrease resistance to blood flow.

Primary hypertension: See **essential hypertension**.

Prognosis: A prediction of the course a disease will take and chances of recovery.

Prostacyclin: A chemical in the body that acts as a vasodilator; that is, a blood vessel opener.

Pulse pressure: A figure that indicates the difference between the systolic pressure and the diastolic pressure.

Renal artery stenosis: A narrowing or obstruction of the kidney's artery.

Reserpine: A chemical used as a sedative and tranquilizer, and for the control of high blood pressure; derived from the dried root of any of the genus *Rauwolfia*.

Retina: A membrane at the back of the eye, it receives the images passed into the eye through the lens and sends them, via the optic nerve, to the brain. It is the only place in the human body where the arteries and arterioles can be looked at directly to see if any damage indicative of hypertension exists.

Secondary hypertension: High blood pressure caused by some underlying disease or ailment. By eliminating the physical cause of secondary hypertension—for example, a kidney problem—it is often possible to bring the elevated blood pressure back to normal. In this way, it is unlike primary (essential) hypertension, which has no discernible cause.

Sleep apnea: An occasional, temporary stoppage of breathing while asleep, as a result of a failure of the autonomic nervous system to regulate the breathing. It leads to several conditions, among which is high blood pressure.

Sphygmomanometer: The device most commonly used to measure systolic and diastolic blood pressures. Also known as the blood pressure cuff, it allows notation and comparison of blood pressure levels by giving those levels values on a scale measured in millimeters (mm) of mercury (Hg).

Stepped care: A method of antihypertensive drug therapy that starts a high blood pressure sufferer on a low dose of a family of drugs and builds up dosage gradually in that and other drugs until control of pressure is achieved.

Stroke: A cerebral vascular accident wherein a ruptured or blocked blood vessel prevents blood from reaching important portions of the brain, leading to brain damage and subsequent debilitating conditions including paralysis and often death.

Sustained hypertension: A description of high blood pressure that stays at the same high levels all the time and does not fluctuate to any important degree, as does labile hypertension.

Syncope: Fainting, as a result of insufficient blood flow to the brain.

Systolic: That measurement of blood pressure when the left ventricle contracts and the blood's force against the vessel walls is at its greatest strength. It is the higher number in a blood pressure reading; that is, in a reading of 120/80, for example, the systolic pressure is indicated by the 120.

Thiazide: A type of diuretic that works to reduce sodium, chloride, and water levels in the body through increased urination.

Tinnitus: A ringing, buzzing, roaring, or some other sort of noise in the ears that is long-term, distracting, dismaying, and often debilitating.

Vascular system: The body's network of blood vessels.

Vasopressin: A hormone stored in the pituitary gland which, when released, causes the capillaries and arterioles to contract, resulting in an elevation of blood pressure.

Vertigo: A sensation that makes a person feel as though either he or the world is spinning dizzily. It is often caused by high blood pressure or diseases of the inner ear, among other causes.

SELECT BIBLIOGRAPHY

Berkow, Robert, et al., eds. "Hypertension." In *The Merck Manual of Diagnosis and Therapy.* 15th ed. Rahway, NJ: Merck, 1987.

Blumenthal, James A., William C. Siegel, M.D., and Mark Appelbaum. "Failure of Exercise to Reduce Blood Pressure in Patients with Mild Hypertension." *Journal of the American Medical Association* 266 (October 16, 1991): 2098-104.

Braunwald, Eugene. *Heart Disease: A Textbook of Cardiovascular Medicine.* 3d ed. Philadelphia: W. B. Saunders, 1988.

Braunwald, Eugene, and Gordon H. Williams. "Alterations in Arterial Pressure and the Shock Syndrome." In *Harrison's Principles of Internal Medicine.* 11th ed. New York: McGraw-Hill, 1987.

Cooper, Kenneth. *Controlling Cholesterol: Preventive Medicine Program.* New York: Bantam, 1989.

Dorland's Illustrated Medical Dictionary. 27th ed. Philadelphia: W. B. Saunders, 1988.

Gifford, Ray W. "Management of Hypertensive Crises." *Journal of the American Medical Association* 266 (August 14, 1991): 829-35.

Goodman and Gilman. "Drug Therapy of Hypertension." In *The Pharmacological Basis of Therapeutics.* 8th ed. New York: Macmillan, 1990.

Guyton, Arthur C. "Systemic Arterial Pressure and Hypertension." In *Function of the Human Body.* Philadelphia: W. B. Saunders, 1974.

Hellerstein, Herman, and Paul Perry. *Healing Your Heart: A Proven Program for Lowering Cholesterol and Preventing or Healing Heart Disease.* New York: Simon & Schuster, 1990.

Holden, Robert A., et al. "Dietary Salt Intake and Blood Pressure." *Journal of the American Medical Association* 250 (July 15, 1983): 365-69.

Horovitz, Emmanuel. *Cholesterol Control Made Easy: How to Lower Your Cholesterol for a Healthier Heart.* Encino, CA: Health Trend, 1990.

Kaplan, Norman M. "Therapy for Mild Hypertension: Toward a More Balanced View." *Journal of the American Medical Association* 249 (January 21, 1983): 365-7.

Karpman, Harold L. *Preventing Silent Heart Disease: Detecting and Preventing America's Number 1 Killer.* New York: Crown, 1989.

Keleman, Michael H., M.D., et al. "Exercise Training Combined with Antihypertensive Drug Therapy." *Journal of the American Medical Association* 2623 (May 23-30, 1990): 2766-71.

Khan, M. Gabriel. *Heart Attacks, Hypertension, and Heart Drugs.* Emmaus, PA: Rodale, 1986.

Kowalski, Robert E. *The 8-Week Cholesterol Cure: How to Lower Your Blood Cholesterol by up to 40 Percent without Drugs or Deprivation.* New York: Harper & Row, 1987.

Krupp, Marcus A., and Milton J. Chatton, eds. "Hypertensive Cardiovascular Disease." In *Current Medical Diagnosis and Treatment.* 26th ed. Los Altos, CA: Appleton-Lange, 1987.

Kunz, Jeffery R. M., and Asher J. Finkel. "Disorders of the Heart and Circulation." In *The American Medical Association Family Medical Guide.* Rev. ed. New York: Random House, 1987.

Larson, David E., M.D., et al., eds. "The Heart and Blood Vessels." In *The Mayo Clinic Family Health Book.* New York: William Morrow, 1990.

Leren, Paul, et al. "MRFIT and the Oslo Study." *Journal of the American Medical Association* 249 (February 18, 1983): 893-4.

Marshall, Daniel P., J. Gregory Rabold, and Edgar S. Wilson. "High Blood Pressure." In *Staying Healthy without Medicine.* Chicago: Nelson-Hall, 1983.

Miller, Benjamin F., and Claire Brackman Keane. *Encyclopedia and Dictionary of Medicine, Nursing, and Allied Health.* 4th ed. Philadelphia: W. B. Saunders, 1987.

Ornish, Dean, M.D. *Dr. Dean Ornish's Program for Reversing Heart Disease.* New York: Random House, 1990.

Paul, Oglesby. "Hypertension and Its Treatment." *Journal of the American Medical Association* 250 (August 19, 1983): 939-40.

"Salt and Your Health." *Consumer Reports* (January 1984): 17-22.

Schmieder, Roland E., M.D., Jurgen D. Rockstroh, M.D., and Franz H. Messerli, M.D. "Antihypertensive Therapy: To Stop or Not to Stop?" *Journal of the American Medical Association* 265 (March 27, 1991): 1566-71.

Stamler, Rose, et al. "Primary Prevention of Hypertension by Nutritional-Hygienic Means." *Journal of the American Medical Association* 262 (October 6, 1989): 1801-7.

Vaziri, N. D. "Malignant or Accelerated Hypertension." *The Western Journal of Medicine* 140 (April 1984): 575-81.

Vidt, Donald G. "Hypertension." *Current Therapy.* Philadelphia: W. B. Saunders, 1991.

Working Group on Management of Patients with Hypertension and High Blood Cholesterol. "National Education Programs Working Group Report on the Management of Patients with Hypertension and High Blood Cholesterol." *Annals of Internal Medicine* 114 (February 1, 1991): 224-36.

INDEX

essential, 12
exercise and, 19, 50-51
fiber, dietary, and, 28-29
gender and, 14-15, 52-53
insurance, benefits of
    control to, 60
inversion therapy and, 20
labile, 9
life span and, 13-14
magnesium and, 38-39
malignant, 14
meat eating and, 27-28
mild, treatment for, 50-53
oral contraceptives and, 21-24
potassium and, 40-44
primary, 12
race and, 14-15, 52-53
salt and, 30-35
seasonal variations of, 15
secondary, 13
sexual intercourse and, 21
smoking and, 20-21, 50-51
sodium and, 30-35
statistics, 9-11
stress and, 17-18
stroke and, 11
sustained, 9
symptoms, 11-12
treatment, nonmedical, 56-59
vegetarianism and, 27-28
video games and, 17
weight and, 16, 18
weight training and, 20
hypertensive heart disease, 13
hypnotism, 56-59
hypotension,
    Addison's disease and, 54-55
    alcohol and, 54-55
    definition of, 54-55
    diabetes and, 54-55
    drugs, cause of, 54-55
    iatrogenesis, cause of, 54-55
    orthostatic (postural), 54-56
    salt and, 56
    shock and, 54-55
    stroke and, 54-55
    syncope and, 54-55
    treatment of, 56

I

imaging, 56-59
insurance, 60
inversion therapy, 20
isometric exercise, 19

K

kidneys, hypertension and, 13
    stress and, 17
    surgery, 54

L

left ventricle, 3-4

M

magnesium, blood pressure
    and, 38-39
    calcium and, 38-39
    food sources of, 38-39
    recommended daily allowance,
        38-39
massage, 56-59
meat eating, 26-27
mutual aid groups, 61

N

naturopathic medicine, 56-59
nicotine, 21-23

O

obesity, 26
oral contraceptives, 22-24
    hypertension and, 23-24
    smoking and, 23-24

P

peripheral vasodilators, 48
polyunsaturated fats, 28
potassium, blood pressure and,
    40-44
    food preparation and, 40-44
    food processing and, 40, 44
    food sources of, 41
    low, compared to sodium, 42
pulse pressure, definition of, 4

R

racial characteristics, 14-15, 52-53
reflexology, 56-59
retina, 15-16

S

salt, alternatives to, 34-35
    hypertension and, 30-33
    hypotension and, 56
    restriction, dietary, 30-33
sexual intercourse, 21
side effects, 46-48, 50-53
    antihypertensive drugs, 45-53
smoking, hypertension and,
    20-21, 50-51
    oral contraceptives and, 23-24
    renal artery stenosis and, 21-23
societies,
    blood pressure information, 61
sodium, antacids and, 34
    Chinese food and, 34
    drinking water and, 34-35
    exercise and, 19
    food preparation and, 35, 44
    food processing and, 40-41, 44
    foods high in, 34-35, 42
    foods low in, 37, 41
    hypertension and, 30-35
    hypotension and, 36
    labeling of foods and, 34-35
    restriction, dietary, 34-35
    stress and, 17

sphygmomanometer, accuracy of,
    7-8
    types of, 8
    use of, 6
stepped care, antihypertensive
    drugs and, 45-49
stress,
    antihypertensive therapies for,
    17-18
    hypertension and, 17-18
    tai chi and, 56-59
    yoga and, 56-59
stroke, hypertension and, 11
    hypotension and, 54-55
surgery, as hypertension cure, 54
systolic pressure,
    age-related changes in, 16
    definition of, 3-4

T

tai chi, 56-59
tobacco, 21-23

V

vegetarianism, 27-28
vitamins,
    as blood pressure treatment,
    56-59

W

water, sodium in, 34-35
    "soft," and magnesium, 38
weight, blood pressure and,
    16, 18
    exercise and, 19

Y

yoga, 56-59

Z

zone therapy, 56-59

74